CAPTURED IMAGES

by
Yvonne Sparkes

CAPTURED IMAGES

Yvonne Sparkes

Cyberwit.net

4/2 B, L.I.G.

Govindpur Colony,

Allahabad-211004 (U.P.)

India

Tel: 91-532-2541153

E-mail: cyberwit@rediffmail.com

www.cyberwit.net

Photography by Jeremy Allen

ISBN 81-8253-024-5

First Edition : 2005

Rs. 150/-

Typeset by Vaishnavi Enterprises, Kamla Nagar, Allahabad
Printed in India at Astha Associates, D. N. Marg, Allahabad

DEDICATION

This book is dedicated to my two sons David and Jon, family and Friends with my love and thanks for their encouragement and Support.

THE AUTHOR

Born in Feb. 1940 at Barkingside, Essex, England. I left England after the war in April 1948 to take up residence in Long Island, New York, U.S.A. I completed my education and returned to England in September 1958. I married and had two sons Jon and David. David is married now to Gayle, and I have three beautiful grandchildren Daniel, Emma and Rebecca. I worked until my divorce at a Livestock Research Centre, and after my divorce for 32 years until my retirement in a local Chelmsford Hospital. 18 of those years working as a nurse on a Mental Health Assessment Unit for the over 69's. I retired in 2000 from full time nursing.

I have written poetry for a number of years and was encouraged to write at a very early age by my American schoolteachers. I have made many friends worldwide through the Internet where my poetry is placed on various sites of poetry. I have received much happiness from receiving e-mails from people throughout the world telling me how he or she likes my poetry. I was voted Poet Of The Year, 2003 by a group of Poets on a very fine site called "Poetry For Thought". The founder lives in Hawaii and has become a good friend.

Many of my poems have been published in magazines, journals, antholo-gies, Newspapers in Britain, U.S.A, Australia, Canada, Israel, Germany, and India. My various interests include the Arts- music, theatre, films, Hiking and world Travel. I love the natural world and have been fortunate enough to visit Asia, The Middle East, Israel, quite a few countries in Europe, Alaska and North America, and Africa twice- Uganda and Kenya. In 2005 I am looking forward to a visit to the National Parks of India, and to also meet the peoples of India. My fondest memories of my travels have been to spend my birthday with a group of Mountain Gorillas in The Bwindi Impenetrable Forest, Uganda, A Husky Dog sled ride in Alaska, an Elephant Trek in Chiang Mai, Chiang Rai, Thailand, and Whale Watching in Cape Cod, Mass. And at the Kenai Fjords, Alaska. As a deeply spiritual person and a love for our creator God's natural world I found that this proves a wonderful inspiration for my poetry.

The author would welcome emails from readers and comments too.

Email *Yvonne.Sparkes@btinternet.com*

CONTENTS

ANGELS 9

AN ODE TO SPRINGTIME 10

A POET 11

A NEW DAY ON CONISTON WATER 12

A DISAPPEARING WINTERS THEME 13

COULD I BE? 14

COME THE MORNING 15

CALVARY 16

BOUDICA 17

AUTUMNS FAREWELL 18

AUTUMN'S SONG 19

I TRY TO IMAGINE 20

HARM NOT THE BIRD 21

CUPIDS KISS 22

GOD'S ANGELS 23

EILEAN A` CHEO 24

ISLANDS 25

IONA 26

IN SPRINGTIME 27

IF 28

IF YOU DARE LOVE 29

LOVE 30

LINDISFARNE 31

LIBERTY IN NEW YORK HARBOUR 32

LEAVES 33

KAIMENI 34

MISSING THE LAKES 35

MAY I DIE FULFILLED 36

MATURITY 37

MAC GREGOR MY SCOTTIE DOG 38

LOVE'S IRONY 39

MY EPITAPH 40

MY LOVE 41

ON THE HIGHWAYS AND THE BYWAYS 42

POEMS FOR VALENTINES DAY 43

POEMS FOR VALENTINES DAY 44

POEMS FOR VALENTINES DAY 45

POPPIES 46

POVERTY 47

SAD BUT TRUE 48

SEPTEMBER MORN 49

SKYE 50

SNOW SCENE 51

SNOWDROPS 52

SONG OF THE LUPUS 53

SPRING 54

SUMMERS END 55

SUMMERS RAIN 56

TAKE ME TO THE SEA 57

THE DOLPHIN'S EYE 58

THE GATHERING OF THE CLAN 59

THE GIFT 60

THE HOLLY 61

THE HUMPBACKS SONG 62

THE MAGPIE 63

THE MIND OF A CHILD 64

THE ONE TRUE ARTIST 65

THE POET 66

THE POETS PEN 67

THE RIVER 68

THE ROBIN 69

THE SPIRIT OF THE HIGHLANDS AND THE ISLANDS . 70

THE SUNFLOWERS 71

THE TALE OF THE FOX 72

THE WILD GOOSE 73

THE WOODPECKERS SONG 74

THERE IS NO GOD 75

THIS ARCH 76

THIS LAND 77

THIS PLANK OF WOOD 78

TIGGA 79

TWO TREES 80

WE HAVE NO TIME 81

WET WEDNESDAY 82

WHERE DO WE GO? 83

WINTER SUNDAY 84

WINTER 85

WINTERS SCENE 86

WORDS 87

WRITTEN FOR DAVID MY SON 25.3.67 88

ANGELS

There are Angels that we meet
When all around is defeat.
When we find it hard to cope
When at the end of hope
God sends us a loving soul
Who will care and make us whole.

When crushed and in despair
When we think there's none to care
Then you will suddenly seem to find
That person who is kind.

God gives and shows in ways
That will brighten blackest days.
A love that knows no bounds
By the Angels you have found.

AN ODE TO SPRINGTIME

I am walking underneath the bough
White blossom on my right
A feast of springtime in full view
Oh what a lovely sight.
The scent wafts round me as I go
I scarce believe my eyes
Such beauty everywhere, on show,
To capture and surprise
The honey Bees so busy now
Wears little socks of yellow
Gathering pollen left and right
This canny little fellow.
The birds are busy gathering
Their beaks filled to the brim
Such eagerness to quickly build
From materials they skim.
Those little twigs and bits of straw
Weaved in to make a nest
Proves them master builders
And seem to know what's best.
In time, the little naked chicks
Will hatch and greet the world
Life's cycle is complete again
And nature's quest unfurled.
Such hope is born in springtime
As with her lovely face
She gives our world a beauty
And fills the earth with grace.

A POET

A lonely Poet has no choice
But, to show his depth of heart and voice.
Alone he sits and ponders life
When thoughts within and ideas are rife.
Who could begin to tell the tale?
To reach extremes beyond the pale
Or gives his view with such aplomb
And bind up words to make them one?
Though life moves on and passes by
The majority of you and I,
A Poet looks in every way
To bring life's rhythms into play.
Experience par excellence
His rhyme takes on a certain stance.
He is known by flair and his own style
For the mind and memory to beguile.

A NEW DAY ON CONISTON WATER

The misty air hangs in great canopies
Across the land enveloped in a cocoon of white.
Only the faintest outline of the shore is visible
Boats now ghostly bob upon the water.
Mist like a tight elastic band hovers
Impenetrable to the rays of the morning sun.
Suddenly an unseen hand scoops the shroud away.
Allows the sunbeams to reach the dampened shores.
Breaks the silence held within
Giving this new day leave to begin once more.

A DISAPPEARING WINTERS THEME

In a momentary flight
This vanishing of white.
Like a sweet, reposing dream
Disappearing winters theme.
I looked and you were gone
My cold white land, now warm.
In a twinkling of an eye
Saw you change and swiftly fly.
Yesterday we gaily played.
Watching sleds and snowmen made,
Shrieks of happy souls to see
Playing oh so merrily,
We saw those white-capped trees
Felt the chilly, northern breeze.
Snowflakes fell upon our brow
Land on trees, and rooftops now.
So silently this dance,
Would soon our souls entrance.
The canvas of my book,
Transformed where `er I looked.
I felt the very hand of God
Surround the place I trod
Now a vanished memory
Is this vision that I see.
So sad to see it go
With all this beauty that I know.
So goodbye this glorious day.
In my mind shall always stay,
And I will remember true
My winter's wonderland with you.

COULD I BE?

Could I be as lovely as a Tree?
Or grow old just as gracefully?
Will my aura burn from red to gold
When I am very, very old?
Will my trunk be stately and so tall?
Show my finest beauty in the fall?
As in the crispness of the air
Sunlight filters through my greying hair.
How splendid to be forever one
And show my bonnet to the morning sun.
Those golden leaves displayed shall always be,
A blanket on the ground for all to see.
Will I pave the way for winter's day?
Let snowflakes cover all the dismal grey?
Virgin snow for birds to softly tread
Leave footprints in that snowy bed.
Squirrels come and quickly look for food
Amidst the twig, the leaf and in the wood
Buried all around in autumn mist
Where sunlight opens like a humans fist.
In the quietness of the coming eve
Where day and night will join and always cleave,
The earth is quiet and now lies very still
As rabbits come to have their evening fill.
I think that God is pleased and smiles above
To give such knowledge of his bounteous love.
And I will always hold fast to the key
That holds this picture framed inside of me.

COME THE MORNING

Comes the morning
Fair mistress of the dawning
Sets another day.
Pulls the mask of night away.
Causes birds to trill on key.
Sing their songs so merrily.
Greeting light and its new page
On the platform of life's stage.
All creation greets the call,
Some will rise and some will fall.
Some will gain, while others lose.
Some won't have the right to choose.
Still the world turns in its way
Greeting night and greeting day.
In this circle that is life,
Meeting blessings and the strife.
So each page is often set
To the circumstances met.
Yet, with just a hand to hold
In life's story to unfold.
We need not fear the hour.
For with love we have the power.
With this power to see us through,
To greet each day and start anew.
Standing tall we face the light,
Or find the solitude of night.

CALVARY

High on that bleak and lowly hill
My good Lord died for me.
Scourged and beaten, mocked, abused
His ransom set me free.
So much was given out of love
And a way was found for man
This real Passover offering,
Our sacrificial lamb.
I kneel here humbly at his feet
That felt those nails within.
My hand in his is firmly placed,
And resolved to start again.
That crown of thorns that bruised his brow,
Brought forgiveness from his heart.
Can I just give him all my love
To make this brand new start?
A triumph claims this fateful day
And Calvary`s hill was won
And as the empty tomb would prove
This is God's blessed son.
So as I gaze on his dear face
While the Christian worlds rejoice
Our love unites on Easter Day
One heart, one mind, one voice.

BOUDICA

She fought her way through a legion of men
Through the wet marshy land of the Anglian fen.
Her chariot hot foot with a strong heart of steel
And the fires of Iceni burning under her wheel.
This Iceni Queen with the heart of a man
Who held just one purpose to free her homeland.
Those hostile invaders that had raped her dear soil
Would one day be gone and would one day recoil.
Her red hair was flowing, and her steeds at the ready,
To settle this score she must drive her horse steady.
He pawed at the ground and his nostrils were flared
As he snorted at odours, unfamiliar and scared.
She prayed to her Gods and her confidence grew
Her war paint looked lovely just like a tattoo.
For this gentlest of women with the heart of a man
Predestined to rule as her royal blood ran.
She was noble and righteous, so indignant with fate,
That had put all the pieces of war on her plate.
They gathered once more at Camulodunum town
To fight for her life and to fight for her crown.
But, for two days alone did the battle survive
As scores of the townsfolk paid with their lives.
Then by Boudica's hand just as legend decreed
She ended her life to be one with the breeze.
With the breeze she does wander and her chariot flies
Through the fens and the marshland of the Anglian eye.
She will n'er be forgotten and will always remain
In the legends, and the folklore of East Anglian fame.
Her name lives forever and always shall be
Whenever oppression's confronted and a wish to be free.

IN ad 60 Boudica, Queen of the Iceni, a Celtic tribe, led a revolt against the
Roman invaders that swept throughout East Anglia in Britain. There was a
battle in Camulodunum (modern name Colchester) which lasted two days and
she was defeated. Legend has it that Boudica took her own life.

AUTUMNS FAREWELL

In displays of colour her repartee
Becomes and autumns soliloquy.
With blustery winds and dampened air,
To strip her trees and leave them bare.
While she departs I watch and sigh
As leaves in fury dance, and fly.
The colours of an autumn's day
Bring reds and yellows into play.
Would I capture and contain
The reds and fires with damp and rain?
For now she rests in natures box
And lives again by seasons clocks.
So naked trees have now become
The welcome of a heightened sun
And cold crisp air with frosty dew.
Know winter has begun anew.

AUTUMN'S SONG

The dampened ground in shrouds of mist,
Greets frills of rain just like a fist,
And tightly held within her clasp
Until those rays of sun at last,
Shall greet her, and disperse the net,
That holds her beauty oh so wet.
Though soggy days are here to stay,
This colour of her leaf display,
Brings beauty and a splendid scene
To brighten the monotonous green.
So autumn brings forth in her way,
Those natural artists into play
And just before she says goodbye,
Her colours flood the earth and eye.
She is the queen of light and air,
Though springtime reigns as one as fair
But, autumn gives this blazing glory
To the end of our year's story.

I TRY TO IMAGINE

I try to imagine a Monet on high
Where the blues of his paintings
Just colour my sky.
The yellows of Vincent's Sunflowers soon
Will brighten the trumpets of the Daffodil's bloom.
Those clouds, Degas dancers pirouette there for me,
A heavenly ballet so enthralling to see.
The palm trees of Gauguin and the hot tropic sun
Will join this cold earth and become there as one.
Old Rembrandt would paint me a much sombre scene
And Constable will open his new Suffolk dream.
His dream of tame rivers and quiet country lanes
His fields, and his mills, and his lovely haywains.
Canaletto would show me, with his palette in hand
A Gondola sailing down canals that are grand.
Da Vinci would offer his most famous smile
If my imagination could take flight for a while.

HARM NOT THE BIRD

Harm not the bird up on the bough
The sheep, the goats the lovely cow.
Disturb the bee in natural course
You feel its sting and feel its force.
Don't tamper with out beasts or flowers
Or over use our chemical powers.
So much of man in selfishness
Still harms the very things that bless.
Look at our earth and all her fruits
As blessings, giving heavenly shoots.
Like gardeners tend our earthly treasure
Keeping her healthy at full measure.
So all of us must give our best
And honour her, just like a guest
But, for a moment we remain
And life goes on the next shall gain.
What we destroy we can't rebuild
Replace the countryside we've killed.
Think long and hard at Gods green earth
What's all of Gods creation worth?
So teach your children to tend on
When you and I are past and gone
Then we will know deep in our hearts
We have given them the best of starts.

CUPIDS KISS

Hare dare that bird in happy song
Up on the bough sing sweet and long?
While I in broken heart ingest
This sentiment of natures jest.

Oh where this sun so merrily
Would show his laughing face to me
And the world and flowers smell as sweet
As my hearts feelings of defeat.

For now come moon with honour show
Your moonbeams with such pallid glow.
Today I've had enough of this
Remembering thoughts of cupids kiss.

GOD'S ANGELS

For every loss there is a gain
To help you through the endless pain.
Though at the time, no hope you see
Of ever feeling differently.
You turn around to find one day
Another blessing comes your way
As Angels come in different guise
Unrecognised before our eyes.
They make our sad and empty days
Seem changed in very many ways.
They show us caring and concern,
They show us love, and in return
Give back that glow of life within,
To cause the will to start again.
Sent by God these Angels come
In times of sorrow, every one.
So when the needs arise in life,
Through all the sadness and the strife
Greet with a smile each one you meet.
As Angels walk down every street.

EILEAN A` CHEO

Oh Eilean A` Cheo you are dear to me
From your high Cuillin ridge, to you blue shining sea.
The shores and the mountains to my bosom I hold
And this vision of beauty, I gently enfold.
You are full salty smell with a sting on my lips,
And your harbour lies teeming with the fish on your ships.
Green rolling hills, or a mountaineer's climb
With a view over Coruisk that is simply divine.
My pearl of the ocean, and the love of my heart.
May your Otters abound you and never depart.
May the Seals grace your island and bob their wee heads
Above those calm waters as they search the seabeds.
Oh my dearest of islands, your soul lives in me.
In my mind I see beauty of your shore and your sea.
Come play your songs softly and then lull me to sleep
When I die it's your memory in my heart that I'll keep.

Eilean A` Cheo – the gaelic name for the Isle Of Skye, Scotland
Cuillin   – the name of the mountain ridge that is very famous to those
                 mountaineers who frequent Skye. A dominant feature on
                 the island
Coruisk   – a beautiful loch (lake) in Skye

ISLANDS

There is something about and island that tells me I should go
It does not matter what the size, wherever water flow.
Just to sit upon the seashore surrounded by the sea
Where Gulls are crying overhead and the waves crash in on me.
My spirit finds my maker, my soul has found it's home
When often I seek solitude it is to this place I roam.
It gives a time of peace in this busy life we lead
An island seems to touch you and to meet that deeper need.
An island throbs with history under every rock and stone
Those ancient stones still stand so proud, in their timeless pagan home.
The Saints of old have planted their faith that lives there too.
Those crosses tall, all weather's proved, this faith took seed and grew.
All kinds have graced these ancient shores, all creatures great and small.
They found this place of quiet pursuit for their quest and for their goal.
As for me I seek the peace and quiet, and I find it with a smile.
For a love of islands in my heart will stay there for a while.
So I will run when I have needed to find that peace again
There's a welcome on those lovely shores and an island is her name.

IONA

Mighty Kings are buried from your past.
Scots and Vikings side by side
Near your Abbey and Retreat
Ancient Celt and modern faith abide.
A coracle found your sacred shores
A holy man would be your vision bright.
Changing your faith forevermore
Columba would be your guiding light.
Celtic Gods would be replaced
A new faith swept across this land
A wind ever tossed and blown
A storm strong as a grain of desert sand.
From far and near Pilgrims here will come,
Consider you a holy place.
Always until the setting of the sun
Men of faith would come to know your grace.
So Iona of the faithful yearning heart,
I come like a pilgrim of the bygone times
To seek that inner solitude
To embrace all the inner peace I find.

Columba came from Ireland, a Celtic holy man. He left his home because of his involvement in a feud, which caused many deaths, and he was ordered to leave Ireland and win souls for Christ. He turned his back on Ireland and founded a monastery in Iona, Scotland where his little round Coracle boat with twelve follows landed to spread the word of Christianity in 563 AD

Iona is the birthplace of Christianity in Britain.

The Kings of Scotland and Viking Kings are buried in this place. To this day people look to Iona for spiritual peace, and there is a thriving community and retreat there.

IN SPRINGTIME

Who holds the clock when leafy buds burst forth on every tree?
Who causes birds in springtime to sing so merrily?
Who paints the Cherry-blossom alive there on the bough?
And gives this blush of colour to winters drabness now?
What artist's inspiration would paint this lovely scene?
Turning in a moment winters grey to vibrant green?
What gives the clue to sunrise to wake our world this way?
And bring the light before us, to start another day.
The world of colour round us those flowers in full view,
This part of nature's secret plan to start our world anew.
Replenishing the dying, bringing hope unto our soul
Knowing creations is just sleeping and soon will be made whole.
Just look outside your window, see all life begin again.
Come see the very hand of God at work down country lane.
Be strong and be courageous, meet life with just a smile.
For your blessing is by living, and being for a while.
See a world so filled by beauty and know that you are blessed.
As God gives to us in springtime, full knowledge of his best.

IF (based on old Valentine verse)

If I come to you my love
With my heart above my head.
Would you gently lay me down to sleep
In your folds of satin bed?

Or chide me with an icy blow
Like winters frozen smile?
And take the wind from both my sails
To rock me for a while?

Or sing to me my Turtle Dove
To soothe my fevered brow
I long for you each day, each night
And Oh, I want you now.

My passions like a raging storm
Abates to rise again.
I've lost my soul, my heart's on fire
Like a Moth flies to a flame.

Oh pity me for I am lost
Save with the hope you give.
So may your ruby lips brush mine
And cause my love to live.

IF YOU DARE LOVE

If you dare love, for pity's sake
Don't blind the eyes, or cause mistake
Nor prove so true that opened mind
Cannot find joys it left behind.
No, love should hold within each breast,
A moment that survives the test.

And grows each day, just like the tree
Stands strong for all the world to see.
Let not the years or tempests greet
The whiles of passions own defeat.
But, steadfast meet each passing year
With hope, with smiles, that outweighs fear.

LOVE

Love is patient, love is kind
Love is gentle, love is blind.
Love does not account the wrongs
But, lives inside as painful song.

Love endures, despite the storms.
Love remains, when all is gone
To hold this love, a beating heart
Wild pulses like the Dove departs.

You hold this love, no time is spared
To say goodbye, or find the words
And in your heart's an empty space
That time and memory can't erase.

LINDISFARNE

This holy place cut off by incoming tide
Where martyrs lived and infidels tried to hide.
The ruined Abbey, this church of Lindisfarne
Times monuments weathered by the storms.
Gospel of St. Aidan and illuminated book
Celtic heartbeat with the years of toil it took.
Home of Britain's faithful and belief of noble birth
Footsteps trod this sacred soil
Imprisoned in your earth.
Now the new age comes to you
To visit where you stand,
The same sea separates the coast
Division of the land.
The seals still bathe, the birds still wade
As they did in Aiden's time
But, a man who turns his heart to God
Is much harder now to find.

Lindisfarne or the Holy Island is located in Northumbria, England. St. Aidan, a Celtic Holy Man from Iona in Scotland, was invited by King Oswald to start a religious community and to convert the peoples of Northumbria to Christianity. Aidan founded a monastery there. A religious Community survives to this day on Holy Island.

LIBERTY IN NEW YORK HARBOUR

Here I stand my torch holds high your liberty
You poor tired masses and rejected of the world.
My shores will dry your tears and ease your loss
Provide you with a new beginning.
Remember hope that long forgotten dream?
A chance to win where others seem to fail.
Come is scores, in droves, in busy ships.
In peace, and in war I will not forsake you.
My pledge is true.
I stand firm and honour with my humanity
My welcome calls, and my torch will light your way.

LEAVES

Those leaves withered, gnarled and brown
I retrieve from a damp and misty ground.
Then I spied the veins running through the leaf
It awakened in my mind a deep belief.
So similar to our human hands I find,
When age takes hold and memory starts to wind.
This leaf, like hands, gives way to time and age
Shall live again once more on nature's stage.
Look closely how akin to trees we are
More beautiful in old age, a shining star
And wisdom and maturity shines within
To give our world it's beauty once again.
At our life's end we shine our very best
Like leaves with colours put to natures test.
We glow with radiance and a heavenly light
To illuminate our world with pure delight.
So when you see a leaf or hold a hand
Though old and gnarled, it is still very grand.
There is beauty still to see and right on view
Though age has claimed, this glory is still true.

KAIMENI

Kaiment sits and looks at me
His threatening face appears
He puffs his little jets of steam
For Santorini`s tears.
His blackened face is now contrite
No more his angry ways.
He shall, in peace, redress himself
For promised calmer days.
Once thick smoke he bellowed out
And vomited his core
This brunt of unrequited love
That Santorini bore.
But, now he sleeps across the bay
So mended in his ways
Where once he'd broken Fira`s heart
And set her skies ablaze.

In about 1500 B.C Santorini experienced a major volcanic explosion caused by
Kaimeni the volcano. Santorini is a Greek Islands in the Cyclades.

MISSING THE LAKES

How I miss the Lakes, the Lakes
The becks, the tarns, the fells.
The boots in hall, the muscle aches,
The pungent woodland smells.

How I miss the Conifer, the Yew
And scented Pine.
The lofty hills, majestic crags,
The valleys deep decline.

How I miss the winter storms,
The snow on Skiddaws head.
When snow alights the Scafell heights
Adorns Helvellyns edge.

How I miss the peace, the peace
Of this vast glorious place.
Where all my fares and worldly cares
Bide in a gentler pace.

MAY I DIE FULFILLED

Mystic islands, distant lands
Calm green waters, shimmering sands.
Gentle breezes on dulcimer wings
Bring white masts to where mermaids sing.
Sea birds flying, sun filled skies.
Church bells tolling, Angel's cries.
Ancient homes and spiritual past
Call to claim this soul at last.
White stone cottage, call me home
And be my refuge when I roam.

Glad my heart and glad my soul
Fill my mind with every goal.
Take my thoughts in resolute being
Where mind and compass are for fleeing.
Bus or Plane, by all that's holy
Grant me every wish and folly.
I pray when this tired breast is stilled
I die in peace and die fulfilled.

MATURITY

Youth has shed its fickle face
By genteel manner is replaced
Where once the goal was wanton plot
And all the mischief it begot.
Those youthful whiles of selfish thought
Changed with the years that life has taught.
There is a joy and peace with age
That takes its place from centre stage
Not now obsessed with wealth or fame
Or conquest of life's fraudulent game.
We are content to breath God's air
Without a worry or a care.
A wealth those greying locks soon know
This wisdom there persona shows.
So age and sentiment deem fine
The products of a life divine
And children look to wisdoms guise
To test the knowledge in our eyes.

MAC GREGOR MY SCOTTIE DOG

A nose like a shovel, a tail like a brush
You are constantly looking for things in a rush.
As black as the coal, with a strange tint of red
You have two cocked ears, on top of your head.
You are wee, and you're funny, you are comically mad
You are my best friend when I'm feeling sad.
Mischievous and clever and so bravely bold.
So ready to fight for the love that you hold.
As you lay by my feet, I know I have a friend,
Who will stay by my side till lifes journey shall end.
That we chose one another MacGregor I'm proud
And where dogs are concerned you stick out from the crowd.
But, I am hoping I have you for many a year
When God calls your name I'll for sure shed a tear.

LOVE'S IRONY

When furnace flames with passion rise
And sparks break out to reach the eyes.
Wild pulses throb to rhythms wild
Then life begets old Cupids child.

When kisses touch those very parts
That senses find in tender hearts
Then nature scores her win and proves,
We all succumb to passions grove.

We cannot hide from loves cruel end
Or when hearts break find glue to mend.
Yet, fate and all who caused the sting,
May one day reap what love can bring.

For now we must enjoy ourselves
Before old age and lust are shelved.
Those memories steeped within our past
Will claim our tortured souls at last.

MY EPITAPH

The passions of my youth have had their day
And all those games of love that I would play.
A dalliance or two would then begin
With luck, I thought, would always see me win.
Now resigned to sickle compass time
I've written down those passions in my rhyme.
Acknowledging a fantasy or two
Putting hopes and dreams in poems new.
Some may read and shed that heart felt tear
Recalling misspent youth and yester year.
Do I feel a sadness in this quest?
Of getting all this knowledge of my chest?
Or say alas, alack and woe today
Rue the morning or curse another day?
Oh no, I smile for memories are rife
Deeply pierced as sharp as any knife.
This life of mine would never bring regret
Show me anything I sooner would forget.
When I'm alone to dream of times gone by
Remembering distant shores where I would gladly fly
Pursuing all those vain and wild desires
When I had need to light my youthful fires.
Now I'm content to stay with home grown scenes
Rolling countryside, resplendent greens.
In these new sewn passions I have found
My wings are clipped and I have come to ground.
Maturity has brought with it a gain
Though I have sometimes known a life of pain.
I'm glad I live and lived life to the brim.
Experienced all the moments of my whim.
I have been lucky and count myself as blessed
To stand here firm until the final test.

MY LOVE *

Oh, my dearest one's a flower so rare
That is born of summer in her hair.
Oh, her song that keeps refrain a part
Sweet tune of love played in my heart.

An Angels face she does impart
To keep within my loving heart.
And I will love her all my life,
Through all the good and all the strife.

Through all the good and all the bad
Till all life dies and happy is sad.
My love for her will never die
Though grains of sand with time shall fly.

For now I bid a fond farewell
When I'll return I cannot tell
But, come again I surely will
Though miles will separate us still.

* Written as a compliment to Robert Burns My Love Is Like A Red Red Rose.

ON THE HIGHWAYS AND THE BYWAYS

On the highways and the byways
In the crevasses beside.
Are the flowers sprouting brightly
With their faces open wide.
You can see the splash of colour,
Golden yellows, blues or reds
As dear nature nurtures seedlings
In the confines of their beds.
She finds those little hollows
In the places we behold
In the cracks of concrete openings
Or those little grassy folds.
The wealth of her pure genius,
Is a sight so rife in spring
As she covers all the wasteland
Where the Robin loves to sing.
No place will she leave empty
Whether great or whether small.
As to greet this radiant colour
Is to answer Natures call.
There is hope and a believing,
That within so small a space
The very hand of God is working
Reflected in this place.
So take a breath and wonder,
Just count yourselves as blessed
As to see this realm of beauty
Is just nature at her best.

POEMS FOR VALENTINES DAY

Come to me my Turtle Dove
Let's bill and coo, show me your love.
My trembling heart in hopes awaits
That we unite it is our fate.

I cannot sleep for restless dreams
To have you is my only scheme.
I stand here holding pleasures cup
Let those red lips partake and sup.

I see your form so fair and true.
It gives me such a wondrous view.
I bow in homage to the one.
Who moves my stars, becomes my sun.

If nature gives so fair a face
Adorns the being with such grace
Then I would find a place to sleep
Your image I will gladly keep.

So kiss me dear my senses reel.
T`is Cupids arrow that I feel.
Your kiss will prove that you had felt,
This passion in my heart and melt.

POEMS FOR VALENTINES DAY

I dreamed I held you in my arms
Besotted by your many charms.
As perfumes filled my nose and rare
Pervading senses and the air.
My hands reach out to touch your form
My fingers seek, your body warms.
I find those crevasses of love
That melds around my hands like gloves.
This touch of flesh makes inner fires
That throbs and echoes of desire.
While fantasy gives reign and plays
Encompassing your form and grace.
Come rock me gently to loves song
Where Venus and her heart belongs.
This passion that is old as time
In pleasures prove just as sublime.

POEMS FOR VALENTINES DAY

Come to me my precious love
Let your passions pleasures prove
And not withheld from tempests whiles
Lead this heart to your beguiles.

Your black eyes burning with desire
Fills my being with a fire
And the source and spark therein is you
Every time you are in my view.

My pulses throb, my senses rise
Temptation's offered to my eyes.
Come kiss and start old Cupids flame
Though souls are lost to Devils gain.

Come bed me now my dearest one
For I am lost, desires begun
When passion's spent we lay entwined
If love's denied will you be kind?

POPPIES

Between the grains the Poppies grow,
With bright red faces, row on row
And give their bodies to the breeze
To tantalize the eyes and please.

This carpet like a setting sun
Spreads out its blanket, becomes one
As far as human eyes can see
A blood red show in front of me.

So many artists try and capture,
This moment held in nature's rapture
When Poppies give their scarlet faces
To our lovely country places.

Poppies come and Poppies go
Give summer such a splendid show.
She is my flower of the fields,
When nature gives abundant yields.

Then dormant she will lay again
Beneath the soil in country lane.
Twixt snow and hail, or rain and sleet
No tempest causes her defeat.

Her will to shine still plays her tune
Her majesty to blaze in June
And ever more this flower will be,
The dearest one of all to me.

POVERTY

There is a poverty of mind and poverty of soul
A poverty of spirit and a poverty of whole.
What is your lonely burden that you walk with today?
Blotting out the sun, and blotting out the rays?
We dwell with abject sorrow, a fleeting peace to feel.
We cannot know what lies ahead, nor touch all that is real.
The only thing to find our way is to plant that mustard seed
To comfort all that inward pain, and to fill that deeper need.
Though we cannot know the reasons, this peace flows deep within
By faith we can move mountains and to start our lives again.

SAD BUT TRUE

A path of glory is n`er long
Remembering our great heroes song.
Yet, evil would so often be
Alive in annals of history.

So sad that good would often die
And deeds of Angels with them fly.
As this poor world of strife and woe
Is bathed by evil's afterglow.

So much was given, tried and lost
By millions who have felt the cost
And what is left? What have we learned?
That bad lives on, and good is spurned.

SEPTEMBER MORN

I can't forget that morning's rise
When flocks of Geese first met my eyes.
Just as my sleeping world was dawning
And a bright new day was yawning,
V shaped columns framed the light
Calling Geese in sunrise bright.
I heard the noisy call begin
When woken by cacophonous din.
I rushed out quick to see them fly
Brent Geese just covering the sky.
There were so many of them there
The sky was filled with goosy flair.
I stood in awe of such a scene
It was surreal, a natural dream.
I watched as each came landing fast
Like airplanes rudders down at last.
So comically they pulled full stop
And landed with ungainly hop.
I watched as busily they ate
Without a knife, a fork or plate
And I shall count myself as blessed
That I was there as honoured guest.

A flock of Brent Geese landed in a field , early one morning, while I was on my holiday in The Island of Lewis, in Scotland. I shall never forget that wonderful sight on a September morning, 2004.

SKYE

Oh to see the misty Isle
From on the ferry crossing the Kyle,
And oh to stand beside the loch
Amidst the baaing, bleating flock
And walk Dunvegans lovely shores
To Coral Beach forevermore.

Oh to see those Cuillin Hills
Black and rugged, clouded still
And see the hills of granite red
Towering above my head.
The purple heather lying there
Surrounds Sligachan everywhere.

Oh to hear the Eagles cry
The Oystercatcher flying by.
To see those Seals on island homes
With young that are not fully-grown
And watch the Otters at their play
Around the lochs and in the bay.

Oh to watch the dawning light,
On Bracadale the sunset bright
To see those shafts descend upon
The Tables Of MacLeod beyond
And feel a certain comfort there
Surpassing mundane life and care.

The Isle Of Skye used to be served by a ferry from The Kyle Of Lochalsh but, sadly that is now stopped and a Bridge has joined Skye to the mainland. This poem was written when it was truly "Over the sea to Skye". And I have fond memories of travelling this way.

SNOW SCENE

A pallid sky tells me that snow
Will soon be falling now.
In flurries carried by the wind
To cover all this ground.

The frozen ground appears pure white
My eyes survey the scene.
Reflected by a pale moonlight,
All ghostly white and clean.

I watched snow fall and saw the change
Transformed before my eyes.
A winter wonderland unfolds
Like magic from the skies.

I looked and in a twinkling there,
Saw every plant and tree.
All dressed in white, this bridal gown
For everyone to see.

Where once a grey and dismal land
In winters grip so tight.
Now changed into a masterpiece
An artist's work by night.

A lesson here I learned so well
That in life's bleakest days.
A blessing shows itself to us
In many different ways.

SNOWDROPS

Upon this frozen winters ground
A clump of Snowdrops I have found.
Their little heads like bells of white,
Just bob the breeze for my delight.
They dance and catch the cold crisp air
Entrancing all who wandered there.
With each movement fairy chimes,
Would ring their songs of sunnier climes.
To think this lowly patch of land
Would offer me this vision grand
But, as for now old winters grip
Seems not to lose her stormy whip.
Yet, recompense is surely there
When Snowdrops dance without a care.

SONG OF THE LUPUS

Song of the Lupus, song of the night.
Howling in moonlight, ever so bright.
To whom do you sing, my slinky grey friend?
What spiritual message are you hoping to send?
With your grey head uplifted you howl to the sky,
With your mournful crescendo ever trailing on high.
In the realms of the forest, you were born there a king
In the glorious moonlight, with the songs that you sing.
So sleek and so grey, so beautiful you seem
Like the spirit of passion in an Indians dream.
So loved and so hated, so feared yet admired.
So filled are our legends, with those stories inspired.
If one of Gods creatures has been badly maligned
Through the ages, dear Lupus is the one that I find.
Such a beautiful creature that brings so much pleasure
By his presence and worth, such a natural treasure.
So let us remember whenever we hear his song
In that forest, at night time where he does belong.
His origins are older, much older than mine
And a place in this universe, he deserves for all time.

SPRING

Today I heard the Robin sing
I saw the very hand of spring.
Up on the bough the blossom burst
And newborn leaves have quenched their thirst.

The day was gentle like the rain
Adorning this quiet country lane.
I walked so softly lest I tread,
On some awakened flowerbed.

The bulbs like spears, thrust through the earth,
To signify a brand new birth.
Such hope appears within the heart
This drab of winter will depart.

When all these colours flood the scene
Encapsulated by the green
Our hearts will quicken to the day
That brings this beauty from the grey.

SUMMERS END

The grapes are ripe high on the vine
The fruit is on the bough.
The air does mist in early dawn
And autumn feels close now.
The harvest's baled, those fields of gold,
Activity is high.
And Swallows gathering on the wire
Soon all will southwards fly.
The Spider spins her silken webs,
And chandeliers are strung
On hedgerows hang these little gems
To greet the morning sun.
The summer storms still rumble on
Humidity is high.
The lightening flashes overhead,
Electrifies the sky.
And yet, we must soon bid farewell
To greet our autumn chill.
Though signs of summer shall be there
Surround our vision still.
Old years do pass and quickly face
Though memory remains
And meadows gold will come again
To live in sweet refrain.

SUMMERS RAIN

Walking in a summers rain
Down a winding country lane.
The rain falls gently on my face
Upon the leaf in soft embrace.
So soft it hits the target true
Wet blanket covering all I view.
Smiling are the flowers there,
They gathered raindrops in their hair.
They nod and wave their leafy stems,
To gather up these moisture gems.
The sun peeps out behind a cloud
His rays soon warmed the dampened shroud
And then my eyes did feast upon
A rainbows arc just further on.
How beautiful this world had seemed.
Just like the loveliest of dreams.
All memory's stored for quieter thoughts
Recalling happiness it brought.
When I sit down and feel alone,
Remembering all that nature's shown,
New faith springs forth each time I see
Those rain clouds gathering there for me.

TAKE ME TO THE SEA

Take me to the sea again
Let me hear the seagulls cry
Let me feel the cool of the oceans breeze
And the sun from a clear blue sky.

Let me watch the sails on the tall white masts,
That greets the sun kissed morning.
While the rough seas break over painted bows
As they skin the oceans foaming.

Lest me taste the salt thrown by hostile seas
For the waves boom on like thunder.
There the sea birds fly in the open sky
And my heart abounds with wonder.

THE DOLPHIN'S EYE

Have you ever looked into a Dolphins eyes?
For you can mirror in them your very soul.
Their deep, intense and profound gaze within
Sees you as no other has before.
She knows you better than you know yourself.
She searches all your private thoughts and then,
Questions deep within your psyche start to rise
As she begins this depth of search again.
All knowing Dolphins of the deep.
In realms and legends were revered
Possessing special qualities they've shown
So through the ages had become endeared.
Now the Dolphins struggle is too plain.
For man has offered her his selfish greed.
Nets, pollution and a captive plan
Is the only fate for our poor Dolphins need.
So change we must and come to know respect.
None looks finer than she looks today.
This poor sad world would never be the same,
If by extinction she would go away.

THE GATHERING OF THE CLAN

Swallows, Swallows everywhere
Up on the wire and in the air
Chattering, flying, swoop and dive
Congregate to keep alive.

Soon they fly away from cold
Veering southwards fly tenfold,
And steer by inner compass they
To find their path, to find their way.

Look to the right, look to the left.
Look in the hollows and the cleft.
Gathering here and gathering there,
Gathering clans meet everywhere.

By whose signal do they fly?
Into the blueness of the sky
But, now they practice trial runs
By the light of the setting evening sun.

THE GIFT
(A Tribute To Poets Everywhere)

I have a gift, the gift of words
That flies without like flocks of birds.
Like birds they fly to freedoms ring
Escape with all those rhymes they bring.

Those fruits of labours so divine,
Like Claret or a fine red wine,
So filled with natures rich bouquet
The poems written still today.

Let pen be poised and quill be sharp.
Let flute announce and strum of harp.
This gift bestowed on chosen few
Gives beacons to the world anew.

And beacons light this cold dark world
When all the rottenness is hurled.
Then poems shine like works of art
To bring that meaning from the heart.

THE HOLLY

The Holly loves the colder climes
Red berries are her dress.
But, only snowflakes are her friends
The cold air her caress.
Her leaves are sharp, unfriendly too
Not for the touch, only for view.
Yes, she is proud and in her way,
So beautiful on Christmas Day.
In decoration she adorns,
The searing cold of winters morn.

THE HUMPBACKS SONG

Who can hear the Humpbacks song?
He sings to his loved one all night long.
Beneath the deep his love song goes
Over the ocean in sonar flows.
His courtship takes him many miles
He hopes his song, a mate beguiles.
He has this yen to pair and mate
But, what of baby Humpbacks fate?
Chased and harpooned in the past
But, still the persecution lasts.
Yes, men still talk about his lot
While carcasses of Whales still rot.
Pretending it's our human right
To hunt him down and kill on sight.
The ones who care fight hard and long
To rectify what man does wrong.
Can the world just leave alone?
What God has by example shown?
A creature fine and learned he
A master of the open sea
Just let our Humpback have his say
And hearts of men in conscience sway.
Our sea and empty place would be
Without a breeching Whale to see.

THE MAGPIE

Black and white bird with the serrated wings
The portend of troubles and the sorrow it brings.
If you doff your hat quickly and a greeting is used
The power is given to dissipate the news.
If two birds are spied then joy will soon follow
As you greet the new morning, as soon as tomorrow.
But, if three of them fly on to your garden gate,
Then a lady will enter your life as your fate.
Four birds mean a male, claim some silver with five
Will six bring gold offerings into your life.
Will seven is a mystery that will never be told
A secret that someday your life may untold.

THE MIND OF A CHILD

The mind of a child is an innocent mind
A mind that is constant and true
And when you are given the love of a child
It produces a blessing for you.
No friend is truer, accepts all your faults
And loves you the way that you are.
In constancy ever and a dear honest face
Is a beauty the world cannot mar.
So dear are these cherubs from heaven above
They give without profit or gain.
The love that they show shines on all who receives
Like the showers of heavenly rain.
When the world takes a toll and doubts creep therein
As you search both the highs and the lows
Look in the eyes of your children to find once again
This love that will make your life glow.
Hold fast to this love and do nurture it well
Your children are gold to your heart
And though you grow old in the measure of time
Their affection will never depart.

THE ONE TRUE ARTIST

If my mind could paint pictures without a brush
I would dab all the speckles on the fine Thrush,
And colour the autumn with gold's and with reds
Paint the breast of the Robin and the Woodpeckers head.
I would gather the flowers to paint one by one
With the colours of rainbows that appear with the sun.
I would flood all the heavens with a radiant blue
Big cotton wool clouds, and bright sunshine anew.
I would give every season a special new look
That will stay her forever in my natural book.
But, sadly no artist with talent am I
But, I can see pictures within my minds eye.
I open them all whenever I'm feeling low
Find this beauty of nature that she always shows.
So grateful I am to be able to see
The master at work and some real artistry.
To appreciate all this creation is fine
And to think all this beauty is yours and is mine.
In a land filled with colour I am truly blessed.
To be able to savour the world at its best.
So I honour the artist who paints every nation
Thank our God for this beauty and for his creation.

THE POET

Why did God the Poet make?
Was it grand design or some mistake?
A blessing or a curse to be
This walk in heart and minds beauty.

Forever seeing hope, despair
The joy in God's creation there
And find the words that reach the soul
Impart the empathy as goal.

The Poet sings his songs of pain
Of unrequited love, and blame
But, when he just bursts forth with tune
The world shall shine, the flowers bloom.

A Poet has such watchful eyes
Forever looking to the skies
He's brought down Emperors and Kings,
And Maidens with the songs he sings.

Such power in the Poets breast
That gives him little peace, or rest.
Forever thinking that his muse
Has left him and becomes bemused.

At night he tosses and he turns
Looking for the words he years.
A masterpiece that lives forever
Or just quoted and misquoted ever.

Poor Poet are you lifes own jest?
Or creation at its very best?
The pen deems mightier than the sword.
From where does spring your passionate word?

THE POETS PEN

If the Poets pen were dried
The words inside forever died.
A sad and empty place t'would be
No rhyme or reason left for me.
To see the world through a Poets eyes
Is to touch the infinite, see the skies.
To gather moonbeams in the night
Or net the stars that shine so bright.
To right the right, or right the wrong
To sing of love in bitter song.
As Poets feel, and Poets curse
Forever putting thoughts in verse.
The sword is weaker than the pen
Inflames the passionate hearts of men.
So Poets give this passionate heart
Eternal words, a place to start.

THE RIVER

She ebbs and she flows, and meanders awhile.
Each bed and each curve, she knows how to beguile.
She kisses each body and foot as it dips.
Or the wings of the wild birds, the bow of the ships.
She is quiet or she's lazy, her mood is serene
Or a turbulent foe, an adventurers dream.
With rapids she rushes, her destiny true
With a foam at her crest, and a wild angry view.
She shines in the morning, and glows with the night.
The sunset gives colour to her waters now bright.
The full moon resplendent shall shine and adorn,.
Embracing with shimmers and caressing her form.
The dulcimer breezes or tossed autumns winds
Shall rustle her waters, cause her to distend.
She covers the earth and in fullness of time,
The seasons and gravity, become her design.
She is pulled hither, thither, and this way and that.
She is long and she's winding, she is thin or she's fat.
Oh wonder of wonders, who gave her this face?
Then gives her such power, such force and such grace?

THE ROBIN

A blush of red adorns your coat
Oh maestro of the warbled note.
In song you stand at heavens door
With tunes the very soul implores.
How can a hardened heart remain
Without a falling tear to claim?
Through weather's good or bad you sing
Remind the listener of spring.
Perhaps to give a faith of kind
That summer is not far behind.
So sing my little feathered friend
Hope and joy in song you lend.
Faith and trust that come what may
There will always be a brighter day.

THE SPIRIT OF THE HIGHLANDS AND THE ISLANDS

Never to roam, may my spirit remain
And fly over hills and over the plain.
Make me part of the wind, that brings summers breeze
To the grass, and the flowers, to rustle the trees.
Let me soar like the Eagle that greets sunlight's quest
With a welcome of friendship, to the mountains a guest
Let me rest of a hillside, and bathe in the streams
By the cool of peat waters, in my island of dreams.

I am one with the earth and one with the sky
On the back of the seabirds, to the sea I shall fly
And follow the boats as they haul their nets filled,
With the fish that are jumping hoping some over spill.
I walk with the Shepherd as he checks on his sheep.
While his dog is up circling on a hill that is steep.
In the corries I wander and beneath the crag
Are the home of the Hind, and the home of the Stag.
The mist swirls and covers the rocks with her veil
And the rainfalls, the ice forms with the thunder and hail.
I am one with her wildness and one with her heart
Let her beauty enfold me so I never depart.

Corrie　– circular hollow on mountainside (Gaelic coire)
Crag　　– Steep or rugged rock
Hind　　– female Deer
Stag　　– Male Deer

THE SUNFLOWERS

They turn their faces to the sun
Seduce the rays and become one.
Their countenance of golden theme
Becomes an ardent lovers dream.
So proud and tall they stand on view
Adorns the ground on which they grew.
Asked adoration of the eyes
In fields of gold I now espy.
They nod their heads when gentle breezes
Through their bodies wafts and teases,
Giving pleasure in the dance
Where eyes and souls become entranced.
So many nod their golden heads
In natures own great flowerbeds.
I dare not move from on this spot
That time and memory had forgot.
Could beauty show so rich a yield?
As Sunflowers dancing in the field?
Where can I store this golden look?
To live in memories picture book?
Yet. One had found the golden key
To hang there framed in front of me
Sunflowers there to captivate
By Vincent with his daubs of paint.
Now all will see and come to know
The beauty of this golden show
And honoured ever more this prize
Encapsulated by the eyes.

THE TALE OF THE FOX

Listen while I tell you the tale of the Fox.
He's been hunted and hounded and had a few knocks.
He's been chased at full gallop, pursued by the hounds
In fear of his life, over fields he would bound.
On highways he's dazzled and looses his life,
And that's not the problem or end to his strife.
The sprawl is fast growing populations expand
Taking his food and his territory, the land.
Now he roots in the offshoots of human's remains
In gardens, and dustbins and down country lanes.
So sad that a creature so beautiful to see,
Must face all these perils in a wish to be free.
So take just a moment to consider his plight.
As a part of creation, let us join in his fight.

THE WILD GOOSE

The harvest moon now large and translucent
Frames our nostalgia
Glowing in a radiant yellow light
Across this windswept strip.
The wild Geese call and bark, and chatter
To each other for now is their preparation time
To leave these shores.
Their will shall lead to warmer climes
And inborn genes wishing to procreate
Will cause their flight southwards,
As generations have done before them.
Blustery autumnal winds cool the dampened days,
And autumn's skirt is tossed and blown with stubble
Across those barren fields.
Fires of colour and leaves join in this wild dance of air
To greet the tempestuous days.
Such herald's autumn's call.
The Russet apples are boxed, bobbed,
Or gorged in the festive days ahead
Our earth has given of her fruit in abundance
And as in a fantasy at eventide we watch
As Geese fly in their formation across a Harvest moon.

THE WOODPECKERS SONG

Little green bird with the Masonic bill
How you just love to tap and to drill.
How I wish that I could just fly
To see all the sawdust sail through the sky.
Such perseverance in one bird so small
To make your impression of a very big hole.
Yes you reverberate round in this park
With machine gun fire and a very big spark.
Rat a tat tat; your drill seems to go
When will it stop? Nobody knows.
Please tell me this and will you be kind
What is inside that you hope to find?
I am so fascinated and I stand here in awe
Such prowess, in digging the hole that I saw.
With your little red hat, and your green body swinging
While the rest of those birds were just gaily singing
You were making yourself a trunk symphony
Your kettledrums playing so masterfully.
Rat a tat tat, Ravel would be proud
Because you can play drums exceedingly loud.
A master, a craftsman you outshine the rest
As you hit the home and put your drill to the test,
If ever our God gave to one little bird
An inner built toolbox with a drill to be heard,
It is you little fellow and you have my applause
As you can keep drilling with nary a pause.
So continue to drill in your trees evermore
This tapping, this drilling, your woodpecker score.

THERE IS NO GOD

There is no God the wise man said to me
Because of all this suffering I see
The world seems filled with poverty and pain
And all is dying from the acid rain.
Agree I must to his observance true
But, this is what I say to him and you.
I cannot give a valid reason why
Yet, I've seen this crimson evening sky
And dew kissed petals on the summer rose
Her fragrance permeates my nose.
I've watched this change from green to gold
The beauty that each season holds
Painting scenes so beautiful and so grand
From a barren winter land.
Such is creation from high above
Hold a baby and feel that surge of love.
As sunlight glows amidst the raging storm
I saw the beauty of a rainbow form.
I've seen the moon and tides that flow and ebb
A Spider busy at her silken web.
The sky at night that casts a merry light
Forming patterns of a star filled night.
This Universe so vast I cannot take it in
Or find the end of it or even ways to begin.
God does exist or some amazing force
That sets the cosmos on a certain course.
That blueprints life and holds the DNA
And shows the truth and love for Man today.
We must just look beyond the suffering to see
The joys of life surrounding you and me.

THIS ARCH

This natural arch frames path and trees
I walk beneath, caressed with breeze.
Resplendent colours meet the sky
To blend with leaf and fill the eyes.
There is a peace in nature's arms
That fills our lives with all her charms.
When worldly cares make our lives bare,
Fill sight and sound with her sweet air.
So come and walk her leafy ways,
Forever in our hearts these days.
This beauty of her trees will be
The finest thing we'll ever see.

THIS LAND

This land of sun and shadows
This land of mist and rain.
This land that pulls my heartstrings
Down every country lane.

The sheep are in the meadow
The cows are in the corn
And I just love her dearly
The land where I was born.

Her mountains and her valleys.
Her rivers and her stream.
The waterfalls cascading
Down rocks and gullies seams.

The light glides o`er her hillsides.
Those shafts on waters play
And I am one with earth and sky
On this my perfect day.

I've walked on golden beaches.
I've watched the eagles fly
Above my head, so regally,
Their dance just caught my eyes.

Around each place and quarter
Wild flowers grow anew
To fill this land with colour
And give a lovely view.

As long as there's a heaven
On earth I shall be found
In the roots of my dear homeland
Where my heart and soul are bound.

THIS PLANK OF WOOD

To think this plank of wood was once a tree.
How many lovers kissed near you, and carved the names I see?
How many little birds nested high up on the bough.
To raise their feathered families, who have lost a good home now?

What man with axen sharp cut so deep to fell you true?
Leaving just a partial trunk, a remnant that was you.
How in majesty you lived, now sadly you must die
To become that plank, a piece of wood,
In a building you will lie.

But, when I see you now, I will think of finer days
Of the seasons changing your green leaves.
Of the lovers and their ways.
Or the merry games of children as you stood so proud and tall
Yes, this shall be my memory when your past I shall recall.

TIGGA

Little Cat with bright green eyes,
Are you a Tiger in disguise?
As on this sunny, springtime day
So stealthily you stalk your prey.

I watch from windows out of view
And see Big Cat inside of you.
Small fellow with a bigger heart
Just like your cousins prowling part.
You walk across those fields of green
A Lion or a Tiger keen.

Ginger kitty that you are
Your prey across that field afar,
Had better find a place to hide
So quick are you with your cat stride.

A powerhouse of brain and gall
I am amazed, in one so small.
Though smaller cousin you may be
All Tiger when you climb that tree.
A bigger cat by far than size.
Your stature grows before my eyes.

TWO TREES

I saw two trees in fond embrace
Their trunks entwined and interlaced.
They have been so long in fixed abode
They had fused together, and it showed.
As if the very hand of time, stood still,
This picture so sublime
Would frame within my memory
A pure delight and joy to see.
This brought to mind a marriage when,
Two people vowed to be akin
And sometimes life would draw them thus
Or part their ways without a fuss.
But, now and then, occasionally
They would fuse together like the trees.
It is then they weathered every storm,
Though life hurled problems, caused no harm,
As joined together hearts and minds
Embraced the years and intertwined.

WE HAVE NO TIME

We have no time to pause and see
The Fox, the Hare, the mighty Tree
Or see the world in full array
The beauty of this glorious day.
We just let pass before our nose,
The fragrance of the summers Rose
Or honeysuckled perfume fair
Pervading nostrils from the air.
We miss those flights of migrant birds
When honking Geese are often heard
And there above, in patterns fly
Their V shaped columns in the sky.
When the sun's a blaze of glory
And reds and purples are her story
We go our way in blinded fashion
Missing all of nature's passion.
That misty morn of Spiders web
When strung up on the hedgerows edge
Like jewels glistening in the sun
Her misty, dewy, autumns song.
The Rabbit close to eventide,
Comes from his burrow, where he hides,
Feels free to nibble there at last,
Now all activity has passed.
So many dramas turn the page,
Of life in our creations stage
But, we pass on without a look
In natures own great storybook.

WET WEDNESDAY

The day is cold, the ground is wet, precipitation everywhere
My body's chilled. My hands are numb
And dampness frills the misty air.
Of all the weathers I could brave
The heat and cold, the crisp of snow
The damp of rain and gloomy sky
Is worse to me than autumn's blow.
Far worse than her tempestuous days
Far worse than blizzards biting flays
Far worse to me her coverlet
When I am cold, and damp and wet.

WHERE DO WE GO?

Where do we go when our time has come?
When we feel those rays of our setting sun.
Though nobody knows, of this I am sure
There is a peace and joy beyond death's door.
A place of love and a rest from the woe
Letting our earthly pain and our sorrows go.
All tears will be dried from every face.
In the fullness of love and surrounded by grace.
When we are transformed to this new life above
Wrapped in those arms of God's bountiful love.

WINTER SUNDAY

The broad sun of winter
Frozen pavements on my way
To melt the icy earth
In the warmer parts of day.
Cold breathe amidst the slumbers
Frozen petals for a dress
She shows a tattered face
To the cold airs caress.
Yet, in death is her compassion
For this penetrating sting,
Will show the newborn leaves to me
At the rising of the spring.

WINTER

It's winter and the earth is bare,
Gone are the sounds of summer fairs.
Only chilly winds and frosty panes,
Large icicles and frozen drains
But, compensation is a-planned
A winter season wonderland.
When warm white blanket covers earth,
All furry creatures in their berth.
The child takes on his snowball pleasure.
To any child it's natures treasure.
The old will think of bygone days
When horse had drawn a handsome sleigh.
The tinkling of its pretty bells,
Only Christmas card now tells.
But there is still a pretty scene.
The land is beautiful and clean.
Each plant and tree a white cap wears.
Who needs the sun and summer fairs?

WINTERS SCENE

Each tiny little snowflake falling to the ground
Covering the grass of green, white jewels all around
And each well formed and perfect as if nature did her best
To work on pretty patterns, each different from the rest
Transforming winters bare and empty look
Into an artists picture book.
This great artist high above,
Has given beauty to the earth he loves
With palette in hand and inspiration too
He colours the scene for me and you.
So beautiful and clean the countryside becomes
With the reflection of fiery rays of sun
And the plants and trees as sentries stand
To guard the snow-white land.
This cold white winters scene to me
Is lovelier than anything I see.
The giant snowman the child is making
In this panorama breathtaking.
Filling my eyes with amazement
At natures great achievement

WORDS

There are words that wound
And words that heal
The power is in us all.
But, the greatest words you will every hear
Are echoed from the soul.
Words that denote the power of love
That often changes Man.
Makes the world a better place
For us to begin again.
So men of faith take heed of this
Though some seem not to care.
When you freely give this loving then
You will cause a healing there.

WRITTEN FOR DAVID MY SON 25.3.67

Who says there are no Angels?
In this sinful world?
I have a little cherub
With shining golden curls.
And heavens love is on his face
My dearest little lover
He fills my life with charm and grace
I'm proud to be his mother.
It's true he holds a devilish part
And is always up to pranks
But, when the goodness in his heart
Shows love then I give thanks
And when he lays there fast asleep
God's love lies on that pillow.
It's then I turn and start to weep
My darling little fellow.